Swedes

IN WISCONSIN

Revised and Expanded Edition

Frederick Hale

THE WISCONSIN HISTORICAL SOCIETY PRESS

Madison

Published by the
Wisconsin Historical Society Press
Publishers since 1855

© 2002 by The State Historical Society of Wisconsin

For permission to reuse material from *Swedes in Wisconsin*, 978-087020-337-4, please access www.copyright.com or contact the Copyright Clearance Center, Inc. (CCC), 222 Rosewood Drive, Danvers, MA 01923, 978-750-8400. CCC is a not-for-profit organization that provides liscenses and registration for a variety of users.

wisconsin history.org

Photographs identified WHi are from the
Society's collections; address inquiries about such photos to the
Visual Materials Archivist at the Wisconsin Historical Society, 816 State Street,
Madison, WI 53706.

Printed in Wisconsin, U.S.A.
Text and cover designed by Jane Tenenbaum Design
Engraving on page 3, "Cabin by Stream," from WHS Archives, WHi Image ID 69827

13 12 11 10 09   5 4 3 2

Library of Congress Cataloging-in-Publication Data
Hale, Frederick, 1948–
Swedes in Wisconsin / Frederick Hale. — Rev. and expanded ed.
p. cm.
Includes bibliographical references.
ISBN 0-87020-337-1 (pbk.)
1. Swedish Americans — Wisconsin — History. I. Title.
F590.S23 H34 2002
977.5'004397073 — dc21
2002001557
CIP

MEIJER & HOLM.

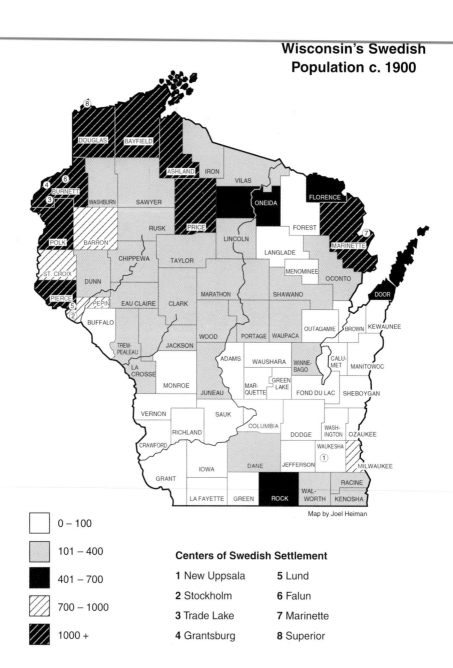

Wisconsin's Swedish Population c. 1900

Map by Joel Heiman

0 – 100

101 – 400

401 – 700

700 – 1000

1000 +

Centers of Swedish Settlement

1 New Uppsala
2 Stockholm
3 Trade Lake
4 Grantsburg

5 Lund
6 Falun
7 Marinette
8 Superior

WISCONSIN'S FIRST SWEDES

In the spring of 1841 a motley group of six young Swedes and one hunting dog sailed from Gävle, Sweden, as extraordinary passengers aboard a merchant ship bound for New York. In contrast to the peasant origins of most nineteenth-century Scandinavian emigrants, three of the four men had studied at Sweden's prestigious University of Uppsala, although none appears to have savored his prospects in the Nordic kingdom. Yet they were even less certain of their future in North America and did not choose a destination until after they had crossed the Atlantic. Three of the men and the accompanying women were to found the first Swedish colony in the New World since a trading company set up shop along the banks of the Delaware River in 1638.

The leader of the party, Gustaf Unonius, came to play a prominent and at times controversial role in Swedish immigrant history. Born in 1810 in Helsinki shortly after Sweden ceded Finland to Russia, he moved to Sweden as a boy and eventually studied law and, briefly, medicine at Uppsala. Upon leaving the university, Unonius took a position in the provincial administration but saw little future in the bureaucracy of his country, whose "age of greatness" was by then only a memory. A self-declared radical, he sought a new direction in his life and, at the age of thirty, married a Swedish lass and departed for America.

Upon arriving in New York on September 10, 1841, Unonius and his friends were assured by an earlier Swedish immigrant that Illinois offered a more bountiful future than any other state or territory. Piecing together an itinerary that would take them up the Hudson River, along the Erie Canal, and across the Great Lakes, they set out a week after their arrival for Chicago, fully aware that they would arrive in what was then the distant American West at a time hardly conducive for undertaking the rigors of pioneer life. Sailing down Lake Michigan, the Unonius party — then reduced to Gustaf, his wife, her maid, a former medical student named Wilhelm Polman, and Carl Groth, a rough-hewn relative of Gustaf — heard encouraging reports about Milwaukee and its hinterland and hastily decided to proceed no farther south.

These Swedes soon discovered that they were not the first of their nationality to set foot in the Territory of Wisconsin. They may, however, have been the first to do so legally. A royal decree of 1768 forbidding virtually all emigration from Sweden had not been revoked until 1840. Nevertheless, as early as 1818 at least two Swedes had worked for John Jacob Astor's American Fur Company in the area, and the census of 1840 tallied at least four Swedes in Wisconsin, three of whom were members of the Friman clan that had emigrated in 1838 from Västergötland province to what is now the Town of Wheatland in Kenosha County. The Frimans occupied a hovel that a fellow immigrant disparagingly found "far inferior to a peat burner's cottage in Sweden." A Norwegian waitress in Milwaukee introduced the Unonius group to the fourth, Oscar Lange, a local hardware salesman who offered his assistance in claiming suitable land.

The following month they squatted on a site along the eastern shore of Pine Lake in Waukesha County, about twenty-five miles west of what is now downtown Milwaukee. In memory of the epicenter of Swedish intellectual and religious life, Unonius and the four other venturesome pioneers dubbed their colony Nya Uppsala, or New Uppsala, at first spelled Upsala in harmony with the Swedish orthography of that day.

Life on the Wisconsin frontier severely tested the mettle of these newcomers, nearly all of whom were quite unprepared for seeking out an existence in nearly virgin forest. Their first communal home, erected in a day after a backbreaking week of hewing logs and hauling lumber, fell far short of the houses they had inhabited in Sweden. In Unonius's words, it initially consisted of "a small unfinished cabin without a floor, without a door, without chairs, table, or any other piece of furniture — only an empty room with great openings here and there between the rough logs." Even after the gaps between the timbers had been chinked and other improvements made, the dwelling proved difficult to heat. Nor did their hay-filled mattresses provide much comfort. Poor harvests from the marginal soil prevented these Swedes from acquiring many of the items for which they undoubtedly yearned, and during the harsh winter of 1842–1843 their diet was reduced to potatoes, coffee brewed from roasted wheat, and, as a substitute for sugar, a foul-tasting syrup they graphically called "nigger sweat." Unonius's wife was in poor health much of the time, and their first child died before reaching the age of four. Their maid married a Norwegian settler in the area but shortly thereafter died in childbirth.

Relations with the Ho-Chunk and other Indians of the region were less a source of consternation to Unonius than they were to many other settlers. Expressing interest in their beliefs and welfare, he joined them on a hunting expedition and visited their encampments but was dismayed when "roving Indian tribes" stole a large stack of hay that the settlers desperately needed for their livestock.

Such arduous tasks as felling trees, splitting rails, and cutting hay occupied many waking hours. Adding to Unonius's misery, his supply of snuff ran out, forcing him to cure his own on the stove using low-quality pipe tobacco that he ground up, mixed with potash, and fermented in a tightly sealed container. Nevertheless, the little band endured these and other privations with relatively few complaints for several years, and indeed the forward-looking Unonius dispatched encouraging letters to the Stockholm daily *Aftonbladet*. Some of their letters were reprinted in other newspapers throughout much of Sweden, Norway, and Denmark. His promising accounts prompted other Swedes (including several of considerable social standing) but even more Norwegians to join him at Pine Lake. (Unonius even played a minor role in stimulating Danish emigration to Wisconsin. Laurits Jacob Fribert, a lawyer from Copenhagen, elected to join his colony in 1843 and four years later published a roseate description of the territory that helped to attract more Danes to eastern Wisconsin.) Generally speaking, the Swedes settled on the east side of Pine Lake, the Norwegians on the west. Some squatted; others purchased up to 160 acres of federal land for $1.25 an acre under the terms of the Preemption Law of 1841.

Yet New Uppsala waned nearly as soon as it waxed. Wilhelm Polman left to pursue his career as a physician in New York, and Carl Groth departed to seek his fortune trading newspapers and tobacco in New Orleans before returning to Sweden in 1858. Some of the privileged Swedes who followed in Unonius's footsteps proved utterly unsuited for the exigencies of the frontier. They complained incessantly about the lack of modern conveniences and, incredibly, the difficulty of hiring servants. Small wonder that Unonius preferred the more numerous and rustic Norwegians of Pine Lake, accustomed as they were to a more austere life in their native land, to his fellow bourgeois Swedish Americans. Yet by 1844 even he had left New Uppsala, though only to study theology at an Episcopal seminary three miles away at Lake Nashotah. Following his ordination the next year, Unonius ministered to Scandinavian and Yankee congregations in eastern Wisconsin and Chicago before returning to Sweden in 1858.

When the Swedish novelist Fredrika Bremer visited New Uppsala in 1850, she found little of the vigor and hope that once had permeated the settlement. "And here, upon a lofty promontory covered with splendid masses of wood, and New Uppsala to stand — such was the intention of Unonius and his friends when they first came to this wild region, and were enchanted with its beauty," she wrote wistfully. "Ah! That wild district will not maintain Uppsala's sons. I saw the desolate houses where he, Unonius, and Schneidau [a former military aide to King Oscar I] struggle in vain to live." The half-dozen Swedish families still there, Bremer added cryptically, "nearly all live in log-houses, and seem to be in somewhat low circumstances."

A few other Swedes settled in Wisconsin during the 1840s, but nowhere did they form distinctively Swedish colonies before the middle of the century. Some found homes near Busseyville (Town of Sumner) in Jefferson County, an area already then better known as Koshkonong and for its growing Norwegian population. They appear to have thrived, but not without enduring the seemingly endless rigors of clearing and enclosing tracts of land. A former teacher from Västergötland, Gustaf Mellberg, betrayed the demands of frontier life in two of his diary's pithy entries for 1846: "June 7th: Married to Miss Juli Etta Devoe by Pastor Unonius at 3 o'clock. June 8th: Split 111 rails."

Two of Mellberg's Swedish neighbors near Busseyville gained more recognition for their labors. Thure Kumlien, also a native of Västergötland, had studied natural history at Uppsala before emigrating in 1843. This younger acquaintance of Unonius almost immediately began field investigations that spanned several decades and made him a recognized authority on the flora and fauna of Wisconsin. He was commissioned to gather specimens for the Smithsonian Institution as well as other museums in the United States and Europe. The second, Carl Gustaf (Charles) Hammarqvist, an immigrant from Östergötland, gained in 1860 the distinction of being the first Swede elected to the Wisconsin legislature.

MASS IMMIGRATION

The lives of these immigrants of the 1840s form an exciting chapter in the history of Wisconsin's Swedes. Yet two important facts must be emphasized. First, there are very few of them before midcentury. According to the census of 1850, two years after it was admitted to the Union, Wisconsin claimed only 88 of the 3,559 Swedes in the United States, ranking it eighth behind Illinois (which led the nation with 1,123 Swedish-born residents), New York, Massachusetts, Louisiana, Iowa, California, and Pennsylvania. Wisconsin's 106,695 immigrants constituted nearly 35 percent of its total population of 305,391, but the overwhelming majority of these newcomers — more than 85,000 — came from the British Isles (with the Irish numerically leading the way) and the various German lands that Bismarck was soon to forge together as the Second Reich. Only a few isolated pockets of Wisconsin were distinctly Scandinavian by 1850. The Norwegian-born population of the state then numbered 8,651 and dominated several smaller communities, while the 146 Danes were spread across at least half a dozen eastern counties.

The scarcity of Swedes in Wisconsin during the 1840s reflects the second important consideration: mass emigration from Sweden did not begin until shortly after the Civil War. According to fairly reliable Swedish government statistics, 3,221 people left Sweden for North America between 1820 and 1849, 2,599 of them departing after 1845. Moreover, many of these early Nordic newcomers, like Unonius, Schneidau, and Mellberg, were well-educated men who presumably could have remained in Sweden but saw their hopes for material success and upward social mobility dwindle as Sweden's once flourishing economy stagnated. Fewer than half of the adult males who emigrated during the 1840s were farmers, while scores were either master craftsmen or journeymen. Sailors, shopkeepers, military personnel, and other employees of the Swedish Crown were surprisingly well represented. Roughly two-thirds of the Swedes who emigrated did so in family units rather than individually, and approximately the same proportion were males.

Swedish emigration rose markedly during the 1850s, swelling the number of Swedish-born residents of the United States and its territories from 3,559 at midcentury to 18,625 a decade later. Illinois and Minnesota attracted the lion's share, while Wisconsin's count rose from 88 to 673, lifting the state two notches to sixth place. Still, the great waves did not begin to arrive until the late 1860s, and they did not crest until the 1880s.

One of Wisconsin's distinctively Swedish communities — Stockholm in Pepin County — dates from the 1850s. Just before midcentury, a native of Värmland, Erik Petersson, emigrated in search of fortune in the gold fields of California. Unlike his brothers Peter and Anders, however, this would-be argonaut never reached the Far West but worked instead as a lumberjack and raftsman on the Saint Croix River. In 1851 he inspected the countryside near Lake Pepin and decided to found a settlement there. One of his brothers, Anders, accompanied a party of immigrants to the area in 1853, and the following year Erik led a group of 280 Swedes from Värmland to America. More than half died of cholera en route, but many of the survivors continued with him to the designated area, upon which they ambitiously bestowed the name Stockholm.

Initially beset by economic woes, this first Swedish settlement in western Wisconsin slowly began to prosper as its residents sold grain, fish, cordwood, and ice from Lake Pepin. In 1857 they erected a one-room schoolhouse that also served as a Lutheran church. Petersson opened a general store and a brickyard, and Stockholm attracted a physician around 1875. Five years later the community's first newspaper, *The Stockholm Advertiser*, began to roll from the press. Communications improved greatly when the Burlington railroad passed through the town in 1886. The following year enterprising citizens convinced the federal government to construct a pier far enough into the Mississippi to provide a sheltering harbor for both the numerous steamboats and the lumber rafts that plied the river.

Curiously, Swedish immigration, which had amounted to only a few hundred annually during the late 1850s, picked up moderately during the Civil War. The causes of this modest increase probably lay chiefly in Sweden, where economic factors compelled Swedes to emigrate, rather than in whatever attractions the United States appeared to offer during its acute crisis. To be sure, it was possible to capitalize on the wartime economy of the northern states, since a labor shortage in the Union enhanced the prospects of employment for newcomers. Moreover, the

Homestead Act of 1862, which gave 160-acre tracts of federal land to settlers who resided on their claims for five years, became known in Europe almost immediately and heightened the attractiveness of America despite the war.

Initially many Swedish Americans, including some in Wisconsin, appear to have viewed the conflagration as a distant teapot tempest of little concern to themselves. Interest mounted as the fronts expanded and it became evident that the Union army could not readily quell the rebellion. Midwestern Scandinavian sympathies, previously pro-Democratic and anti-Whig, had shifted in the late 1850s to supporting Lincoln and the young Republican Party. Most who had any political opinions probably would have agreed with the young Swede in Manitowoc who wrote home shortly after the Republican victory in 1860 that "Lincoln is a shining symbol of what we hope to find in America: unlike most other politicians nowadays, he is determined to champion the cause of freedom regardless of the cost."

As hostilities dragged on, some of the early Swedes in Wisconsin were exposed to the war's ferocity. By August 1862, President Lincoln had ordered the northern governors to draft men if volunteers failed to meet quotas, a step finally taken in November of that year. The Enrollment Act passed by Congress in 1863 required most men between the ages of twenty and forty-five, including those who had not yet acquired citizenship, to register for possible conscription. Like most of their Yankee and immigrant neighbors, the Swedes of Wisconsin found it difficult to raise the $300 exemption fee or locate substitutes to go in their stead as permitted by the act. Many consequently marched off in the blue woolens of the Union armies. Others enlisted voluntarily — more or less — in what they perceived as a holy war against disloyalty and human servitude, punctuating their letters home with dubious comparisons of slavery and the working conditions they had endured in Sweden. Indeed, out of Wisconsin's Swedish population of only 673 in 1860 (reinforced to an unknown degree by wartime immigration), 100 volunteered.

A few joined the Third, Fifth, Twenty-third, and Twenty-seventh Regiments, while the Twelfth went south in 1862 with at least a dozen Swedes in its ranks. The majority, however, signed on with the "Scandinavian Regiment," officially the Fifteenth Wisconsin Infantry, commanded by a Norwegian, Hans Christian Heg. Its other officers included at least four Swedes. Bloody fighting in Kentucky, Tennessee, and Georgia decimated its ranks, killing nearly a third of its troops. "It was the most bestial mess I have ever witnessed," wrote one Swede after the battle of Chickamauga, in which Colonel Heg fell. "Gory bodies were strewn across the fields like fallen timber. Half of the boys in our outfit are dead or dying, but I think we gave more than we got."

The Civil War provides a convenient line of demarcation between the preliminary and the main exodus of Swedes from the Old World to the New. What had been a trickle before Fort Sumter swelled to a steady stream not long after Appomattox. Antebellum Swedish immigration to Wisconsin had been limited and sporadic, failing for the most part to make a permanent imprint on the ethnic landscape of the state. But the mass migration that began in the late 1860s changed both Sweden and the Midwest fundamentally.

Historians have found several causes for the displacement of roughly 1,200,000 people from Sweden to North America. Most of them are rooted in rapid population growth and the upheavals wrought by economic modernization. As in most other European lands, the population of Sweden mushroomed alarmingly during the nineteenth century as death rates — especially infant mortality — plummeted and birth rates remained high. In 1800 there were 2,347,303 Swedes; half a century later the number had climbed to 3,482,541, an increase of nearly 50 percent. Despite substantial emigration, the population grew nearly as rapidly after 1850, so that by 1900 it stood at 5,136,441. On the face of it, Sweden might appear to have been able to accommodate this expanding population because of its relatively large size, comprising nearly 487,000 square kilometers and being geographically one of the largest countries in Europe. (Wisconsin, for purposes of comparison, covers approximately 146,000 square kilometers.) But Sweden is understandably one of the most sparsely populated European countries, since much of its soil and terrain are ill-suited to agriculture, which until the twentieth century formed the backbone of the nation's economy. The Swedes adapted relatively well to the soil as long as their numbers increased at a glacial pace, but the population explosion after 1800 inevitably put immense pressure on the arable land.

Efforts to modernize the nation's agriculture, together with modifications in its land-tenure laws, compounded the problem. During the first quarter of the nineteenth century the Swedish government phased

out its venerable open-field system, which divided arable land into un-
enclosed areas that were then used by different farmers in the neighborhood, in favor of systematic enclosure as part of a strategy to facilitate
advanced farming methods. In many instances the redistribution of
plots compelled smallholders to relocate on forested land, where they
had to grub out fields like settlers on the American frontier. Some of
these domestic pioneers succeeded in transforming their new domains
into viable farms; others found it impossible to make a living. Had its
population stabilized, rural Sweden nevertheless might have managed to
muddle through. But the sharp rise of the population, coupled with the
termination of primogeniture in favor of equal inheritance, necessitated
even more subdivision of the fields. As a consequence, profitability di-
minished still further.

Many Swedes abandoned their fruitless attempts to eke out an existence from shrinking plots and instead went to work for more fortunate
farmers, often under agreements resembling those that American share-
croppers entered into. These trends swelled the landless rural proletariat
to 40 percent of the entire Swedish population by the 1850s, compared
to 20 percent a century earlier. The once-proud Nordic kingdom had
been reduced in large measure to a land of impoverished, dispirited
farmhands. A decline in real wages owing to this labor surplus further
eroded living standards. At the same time, encouraging reports from
North America made many Swedes realize that poverty need not be
their lifelong fate. Not surprisingly, emigration was greatest from those
areas where subdivision had proceeded furthest.

Other dispossessed Swedes sought to improve their lot by migrating
to the cities, especially after the Industrial Revolution reached Scandinavia during the second half of the century and created a demand for
factory workers. Stockholm's population grew from 93,070 at midcentury to slightly over 300,000 in 1900. The rate of increase in Sweden's second largest community, the western harbor city of Göteburg,
was even greater, from 26,084 to 130,619 during the same period. As
elsewhere on both sides of the Atlantic, however, industry in Sweden
lurched through "boom and bust" cycles and proved incapable of ab-
sorbing the steady stream from the countryside. For many Swedes,
therefore, the cities proved to be roadhouses on journeys that eventually
took them to the United States. As the century drew to a close, the number of Swedes emigrating from cities to North America approached the

number that came directly from rural areas and even surpassed it after World War I.

Noneconomic factors played a secondary role in fostering Swedish emigration. One was a stiffening of the national military service obligation. Young men who had not yet been conscripted often found it difficult legally to obtain certificates allowing them to leave the country. As a result, they frequently slipped across the border and left for America from Norwegian or Danish ports. Others purchased counterfeit papers at surprisingly low prices. Emigration to avoid the armed forces became a public secret, a more or less accepted offense that proved difficult to halt. It is impossible to determine how many young Swedes defected in this way, however, partly because the group most liable for conscription — men in their early twenties — contributed most heavily to emigration anyway.

Religious factors were also secondary to economic considerations. The state Lutheran church unquestionably disaffected many Swedes during the eighteenth and nineteenth centuries, yet the overwhelming majority retained nominal membership in it. Others joined Baptist, Methodist, or other nonconformist congregations that had begun to appear as a result of English and American missionary efforts. Both official and popular toleration of these dissenting denominations came gradually but had reached a fairly advanced stage before emigration peaked. Very few Swedes were thus compelled to leave their homeland in search of religious freedom. Still, members of denominations that resulted from successful missionary efforts in Sweden naturally cultivated ties with coreligionists in the United States. Missionary work by Americans also fostered a general interest in the United States, not just in the denominations sponsoring it. Occasionally some Swedes, most notably Latter-day Saints (Mormons), emigrated in groups, in some instances with passage underwritten by American fellow believers. Swedes who settled in Wisconsin represented a relatively broad denominational spectrum, but these immigrants' beliefs do not appear to have influenced their decision to emigrate in more than a few cases.

Wisconsin did not wait passively for immigrants to pour in. Beginning in 1852, it actively recruited them through an agent in New York City, in pamphlets distributed abroad, and in German and Netherlandic newspapers in Europe. Such activities were the first of their kind among the midwestern states, and they were expanded in 1853. Anti-immigrant sentiment was rife by 1854, however, and the Wisconsin legislature voted that year to eliminate the New York office, which closed the following April. Apart from advice and aid given to some Swedes who found their way to its doors, little special attention seems to have been directed toward Swedish immigrants. Most of it was aimed at Germans, Norwegians, and Netherlanders, perhaps in part because Wisconsin's first commissioner of immigration was a native of Holland.

Shortly after the Civil War, Wisconsin again began to recruit European settlers through a Board of Immigration established in 1867. It competed with similar agencies representing other states. Much of the Board's activity involved preparing and distributing on both sides of the Atlantic pamphlets extolling the state's virtues in German, Norwegian, Netherlandic, English, French, Welsh, and Swedish. From time to time local agents assisted immigrants in Milwaukee and Chicago, but not again in New York. The Board struggled financially for several years, and it is questionable whether it played a significant role in attracting many settlers, although it counseled thousands who already were in the state. In any case, its Swedish work always lagged behind it efforts to draw nationals of certain other countries, most notably Norway and Germany. (The presence of Norwegians in leading Board positions may help to explain this, for Norway and Sweden were then in a state of some tension that lasted until the hegemony of the Swedish Crown over Norway ended in 1905.) Unofficially, railroads, real estate agents, and others with vested interests in increasing the population of Wisconsin complemented the Board's activities. Together with enthusiastic "America letters" written by immigrants already in the state to friends, relatives, and newspapers in Sweden, they constituted the most important "pull" factors drawing immigrants from Sweden.

THE JOURNEY TO AMERICA

Swedes who emigrated before the Civil War routinely endured Atlantic crossings that typically took six weeks. Subject to the caprices of the zephyrs, however, the voyages often lasted from two to three months. Passengers usually embarked at Göteburg, although some sailed from smaller Swedish ports. Regardless of where they put out to sea, most early emigrants soon found their shipboard accommodations to be little better than those for the cargoes of iron with which they shared the limited space below decks on masted sailing vessels. Epidemics were common on board, as were burials at sea. To many landlubbing Swedes, the incessant yaw and roll of vessels in the North Atlantic was a constant misery, and lurid descriptions of seasickness customarily filled their first letters home from the New World. "Anne seemed on the verge of death for much of the voyage," wrote one immigrant of his wife in 1849. "She ate next to nothing and could keep even less down. Both of us had diarrhea for several weeks. The stench in steerage was unbearable, but we could do nothing to escape but wait and pray." One of the few consolations for antebellum immigrants was that by sailing directly to North America aboard Swedish ships, most avoided ethnic intolerance and other unpleasantries that often plagued those who left in polyglot company on foreign vessels after the 1860s.

During that decade and the 1870s, transatlantic shipping underwent several transitions that profoundly affected passenger traffic. Most obviously, steam power gradually replaced sails and reduced marathon crossings to relative sprints of about ten days. Furthermore, the larger steel ships were less subject to waves and weather, and reports of seasickness decreased markedly. No less significantly, American, Canadian, and especially British shipping companies entered and soon dominated the Scandinavian immigrant market. By the time Swedish emigration peaked in the 1880s, most sailed aboard vessels on which English was the language of the bridge. They typically crossed the North Sea from Göteburg to Hull, traversed northern England by rail, and, often after an uncomfortable ordeal of several days' duration, crossed the gangplank with 1,500 to 2,000 other impoverished, America-bound peasants from a dozen or more lands.

Like other Scandinavians, Swedes frequently commented disparagingly on members of foreign nationality groups with which they had had no previous personal contact, especially indigent fellow passengers from central Europe. Jews fared especially poorly under the pens of migrating Swedes. "A filthier lot I've never seen and could hardly imagine in Malmö," wrote a single girl on her way to New York in 1892. "They had both fear and depression in their eyes." Irish emigrants also became objects of scorn, and Swedes occasionally reported altercations between them and other passengers. After an already crowded British liner stopped at Queenstown (now Cóbh), Ireland, to take on additional passengers, one Swede wrote that "tensions on board are now at the breaking point. These foul, short-tempered Irish with their whisky and superstitions are a daily source of arguments. Nobody knows when open warfare will begin."

Service on transatlantic voyages varied from mediocre to nonexistent, according to Swedish perceptions. Shipboard rations satisfied nobody, consisting on many vessels of porridge, hard bread, salted fish, and meat long past its prime. Passengers complained about surly crewmembers, exploitative prices for additional food, and mistreatment of baggage. The meager pleasures on board included free rounds of low-quality alcoholic beverages on some lines and, occasionally, entertainment by talented passengers or sailors. Both American and various European governments' maritime legislation regulated conditions eventually and ensured minimal standards of hygiene and space per passenger, but few immigrants from Sweden or indeed any other country viewed the Atlantic crossing with nostalgia.

Fares from Scandinavia to North America generally were within reach of employed Swedes, although the purchase of tickets for an entire family left many Swedish workers and peasants nearly penniless upon arrival in the New World. Competition among the dozen or more lines vying for passengers at any given time worked to the advantage of prospective emigrants. Others were caught in fluctuations wrought by principles of supply and demand. Whenever the flow of emigrants tapered, fares were slashed, but they usually rose again when the flow increased. Through an extensive network of agents and part-time subagents, most of whom were employed in various service occupations and were thus in close contact with the population, the major shipping companies advertised throughout Sweden and made it possible even for those who were ignorant of the work beyond their own parishes to book transportation without difficulty. They merely appeared at a nearby office and stated their preferred destination and date of departure. In many instances, however, relatives already in the United States attended to these details and sent prepaid tickets to kinfolk or others in the old country.

Swedes bound for Wisconsin generally entered the United States at New York, although Boston, Philadelphia, New Orleans, and other coastal cities also served as ports of entry. Nor was it uncommon to sail to Quebec. Many immigrants held through-tickets to midwestern destinations and did not linger in the East. Most who arrived after the Civil War availed themselves of the sprawling railroad network for their journeys westward, again at reasonable fares. Because Chicago served as the hub of the interconnected systems, hundreds of thousands of Swedes passed through that city, with enough of them staying to give it the world's third largest aggregation of Swedes by 1900. Other Wisconsin-bound immigrants continued to use the Great Lakes as their passageway to Milwaukee and other port cities, even after the rails had begun to provide a much faster route at competitive prices.

ON WISCONSIN SOIL

Reports of the U.S. Census Bureau reflect the proliferation of Swedes in the Badger State as the century progressed. To a far greater extent than Norwegians or Danes, they found homes in the western and northern counties. The Saint Croix River valley had begun to emerge as a distinctly Swedish area as early as the 1850s, but this was due to settlements on the Minnesota side. Fertile and to a large degree still forested, the Wisconsin side began to attract growing numbers of Swedes during the late 1860s, especially Polk and Burnett, but also Saint Croix and Pierce Counties. Swedish communities sprouted there in the 1870s and 1880s, some with names such as Lund, Falun, Karlsborg, West Sweden, and Freya to betray their ethnic genesis. Others, bearing less obvious names, emerged at Trade Lake, Grantsburg, Sand Lake, Centuria, Little Plum, Dresser Junction, Clayton, Amery, and elsewhere.

Trade Lake in Burnett County was among the largest of these scattered settlements. A Swede settled there in 1865, the year the county was created, and, lonely for immediate white neighbors, he soon wrote to a Swedish newspaper in Chicago and praised the natural beauty of the vicinity. His hopes of drawing Swedes there were fulfilled in 1868 when a group of miners' families who had recently arrived in the vicinity of Green Bay decided to relocate there. Several Swedes from Chicago also moved to Trade Lake. Practically nowhere, however, did exclusively Swedish towns develop. In most instances these immigrants settled in areas where Yankees, Norwegians, Germans, or other newcomers already had purchased land.

Farther north, Swedes had begun to drift into Superior in small numbers during the 1850s. Many of these were bachelors who had begun to farm in Minnesota but hoped to capitalize on the bustling community's prosperity as shipping from its port increased. The short-lived depression following the Panic of 1857 cost some their jobs, though, and relatively few others came until late in the century. By 1890 nearly 60 percent of the Swedish-born residents of Wisconsin lived in the northwestern quarter of the state. Owing largely to the lumber industry, the northeastern quarter was home to a further 21 percent in 1890. Marinette became the greatest center for Swedes in that corner of Wisconsin.

Pioneers in the northern counties encountered some of the same difficulties in the 1860s and 1870s that Gustaf Unonius and his party had faced at New Uppsala a generation earlier. Because towns of any size were few and far between and many of the settlers arrived well in advance of the railroad, conditions were invariably primitive and necessitated subsistence farming. The resourceful immigrants soon came to terms with the forest, however, and found it to be a good provider. Logs for cabins and other structures existed in abundance. One family that settled near Trade Lake in 1868 built a typical home some five meters wide and nine meters long, divided into two rooms of unequal size. Its bark roof soon cracked and admitted nearly as much rain as otherwise leaked to the earthen floor. "We did not have time to cut and hew planks for a floor, because we had to clear the forest and plant our crops first," explained one of the sons, L. J. Ahlstrom, in his memoirs. He admitted that "the women were generally tired of it all and wished they were back in Sweden where they had both roofs and floors."

The forest and lakes furnished most of the meals before agriculture got well underway, and many of them afterward, too. Swedes found familiar and palatable freshwater fish of several species. The men hunted grouse, prairie chickens, geese, ducks, and deer much of the year. Stories of confrontations with black bears circulated by the score, according to one Swede, and farmers often shot bears that preyed on their livestock, especially the pigs. Estimations of the meat varied. "They call it bear steak," recalled one newcomer who had been invited to a neighboring farm to help consume the result of a successful hunt. "But just as I was about to try my first bit, I imagined the massive jaws and uncomfortably long claws and lost my appetite." Such natural delicacies as maple syrup, wild honey, fruits, and berries garnished many a rough-hewn table. Grapes also grew near many lakes and streams but were too sour to eat. Lacking sugar, the first settlers were unable to make wine. Nor did many emulate the Indians by harvesting the abundant wild rice.

Most Swedes sought to transplant the amenities of nineteenth-century domestic life to the Wisconsin frontier, but at least one hoped to answer the call of the wild to the fullest. "He claimed that it was better to live like the Indians than to lead the hectic life that our developed civilization demands," wrote Ahlstrom. Besides, "their religion and concept of the happy hunting grounds were [supposedly] simpler and easier to grasp." This malcontent seriously considered finding an Indian girl to be his wife. Arriving at Clam Lake in Burnett County, he was escorted by a Swedish settler, August Magnuson of Grantsburg, to the hut of a white man who had taken an Ojibwe bride. "A kettle suspended over the fireplace contained bear meat, of which the man held a piping hot piece on a fork while his better half sat facing him eating the same course, although they could not see what she used to hold her piece. When they came out, Magnuson elbowed the malcontent Swede and assured him that if he were simply man enough to shoot a bear, he could begin his halcyon life whenever he wanted. The woods are full of Indians, and the hunting was even better in the hereafter." (Whatever became of the would-be paleface Indian or whether he had second thoughts is, unfortunately, unknown.)

Relations with the Ojibwe (the predominant Indian group in Swedish-settled areas) and other tribes were generally harmonious during the latter part of the century. Stories of the Sioux Uprising of 1862 and subsequent conflicts in Minnesota and Wisconsin kept Swedes wary for many years, but their fears were for naught. Occasionally immigrants and Ojibwe learned enough of each others' languages to conduct trade and carry on simple conversations. The Swedes tended to view the Indians condescendingly as primitive people corrupted by civilization rather than as enemies. "They were beggars, asking for tobacco and food," remembered Ahlstrom. One of his relatives, a local teacher, received permission to admit nineteen of them to her school. "Some learned to read and write just as fast as the Swedish children. But like their parents, they resisted English." She found it particularly difficult to command their attention all day, and whenever one decided to leave early, his eighteen gregarious comrades would also march out.

Most Swedes in rural Wisconsin were inevitably too preoccupied with carving farms out of the wilderness to cultivate ties with Indians. Much of the land they bought was virgin forest, but later immigrants — generally those who arrived after about 1890 — had to settle for cutover land that lumber companies had cleared and then sold at what seemed to be bargain prices. In either case, countless stumps had to be grubbed out before large acreages could be plowed. Potatoes for home consumption usually were the first crop attempted, followed by corn, often of the multicolored "Indian" variety. Vegetable gardens, of course, were universal. As the forest receded, small grains and other field crops became feasible. Whatever the birds, squirrels, and other animals left untouched was harvested. As in Sweden, settlers cut large quantities of grass hay for use as winter fodder.

Most immigrants soon acquired livestock, although the limited resources of many kept herds small for a decade or longer. Oxen were a necessity for hauling timber, plowing the soil, and other chores. Horses, invariably more expensive, occupied a higher rung of the acquisitions ladder. Many Swedes kept hardy sheep for both wool and mutton as well as a sow or two, whose large litters provided quick returns on investments. With careful breeding and good fortune in the up-and-down commodities markets, it was possible to build substantial herds within a decade or so after arrival. Nevertheless, the marginal soil in northern Wisconsin prevented most from prospering to any great degree through agriculture alone.

EARNING A LIVING

The kaleidoscope of Swedish immigrants' occupations gradually became more complex as Wisconsin's economy matured. These newcomers brought with them a surprisingly broad range of vocational skills, more indeed than their predominantly rural backgrounds might indicate. Some of those who settled in Burnett and Polk Counties had been millers, tailors, cobblers, cabinetmakers, smiths, miners, carpenters, painters, masons, sailors, watchmakers, teachers, soldiers, and machinists as well as farmers. Probably owing to the abundance of inexpensive land, farming initially attracted many who had never tilled the soil in

Sweden. Within a few years, however, many took advantage of the man-
ifold opportunities that prosperity and rapid population growth brought
to the state. Construction of all sorts provided employment for thousands, often at wages higher than could be earned on small farms.
Swedes built roads, constructed bridges, laid ties and rails as the "iron
horse" galloped across Wisconsin, raised barns, houses, schools, shops,
and other buildings, and otherwise helped develop the infrastructure of
the state's diversifying economy.

Heavy industry, on the other hand, attracted relatively few. In 1890
only 320 of Milwaukee's 204,468 residents were Swedish immigrants (in
contrast to the city's 54,776 German immigrants). Indeed, the industrial
southeastern counties of Wisconsin never had more than a quarter of
the state's Swedes after 1870. Only after the turn of the century did
Kenosha, Racine, and Milwaukee Counties have Swedish populations
of much significance, and then only because of internal migration by
immigrants who had initially settled elsewhere. When the 1930 census
was taken, 40.5 percent of Wisconsin's Swedes were classified as farm
residents, compared to 30.2 percent in Minnesota, 18.7 percent in Michigan, and 16.6 percent of Swedish-Americans as a whole. At that time
slightly less than 30 percent of all Wisconsinites were still "down on the
farm."

The expansion of the lumber industry in northern Wisconsin late in
the nineteenth century provided further employment opportunities and
confirmed the northerly geographical distribution of the state's Swedish
population. During the 1880s and 1890s lumber camps near Superior,
Hayward, Marinette, and other towns in the northwestern and northeastern extremes drew Swedes willing to wield saws and axes. The communities themselves attracted both lumberjacks' families and men who
worked in sawmills and related industries. On weekends their numerous
saloons became crowded babels as sawyers and other workers competed
to trade their hard-earned wages for wine and women, if not necessarily
song. Owing partly to ethnic friction, fisticuffs frequently broke out. One
resident of Hayward's so-called Swedetown wrote to his parents that
"the violence is no less embarrassing than dangerous to those of us who
choose to behave ourselves like civilized human beings. Swedes join
lumbermen of other nationalities in carousing through the streets, hurl-
ing not only foul insults but also bottles and other objects about." After
the turn of the century the Swedish-born population of the northern-

most counties waned, partly as a consequence of the decline of the logging industry, but also because members of the first generation gradually died and immigration slackened.

Women whose husbands acquired farms did the chores and endured the drudgery that befell farmers' wives throughout much of the United States until well into the twentieth century. They raised children, grew and preserved fruits and vegetables, gathered eggs, churned butter, knit garments, washed clothes by hand, and often worked alongside the men in the barns and fields. Many Wisconsin farmsteads did not have electrical current until the advent of the Rural Electrification Administration in the 1930s; before then life generally included many hours of daily toil for farm women regardless of their ethnic identification. Those whose husbands supplemented their incomes through seasonal work in lumber camps also bore the brunt of the general chores during the winter months.

Some women became breadwinners by beginning what economic historians call "cottage industry." At Trade Lake, for instance, "they began to knit socks as soon as they could get a hasp of yarn. Before the Olins had any road other than a winding Indian path, Mrs. Olin had managed to acquire a ball of yarn, and once while I was out hunting I met her knitting stockings," recalled a neighbor. He added that "the wares produced by the women of Trade Lake were never exported, however, since the local demand for them was so great."

Unlike Swedish girls in American cities, not many in rural Wisconsin appear to have sought jobs as maids and governesses. No doubt part of the explanation is that small towns had few such positions to offer. Girls of the second generation, though, frequently aspired to careers as elementary school teachers, nurses, and in other occupations then regarded as distinctly female.

WHi Image ID 69863

A home in Sweden, typical of the working class (date unknown). Until 1840, virtually all emigration from Sweden was illegal by royal decree.

WHi Image ID 69864

Swedish homestead (date unknown). Life on the Wisconsin frontier was difficult for
early Swedish immigrants, most of whom were unprepared for carving out homesteads in the area's wild, heavily forested lands.

After the mid-nineteenth century, advertising handbills like this one beckoned Swedes to America. By 1860 the number of Swedish-born residents of the United States and its territories had reached 18,625.

WHi Image ID 69868

Gustaf Unonius, self-declared radical and founder, in 1841, of one of Wisconsin's first Swedish communities, New Uppsala, along the eastern shore of Pine Lake in Waukesha County. Unonius ministered to several congregations in eastern Wisconsin and Chicago before returning to Sweden in 1858.

WHi Image ID 69869 WHi Image ID 45953

Left: Carl Gustaf Mellberg, a schoolteacher from Västergötland who settled near Busseyville (Jefferson County), recorded in his diary for 1886: "June 7TH: Married to Miss Juli Etta Devoe by Pastor Unonius at 3 o'clock. June 8TH: Split 111 rails." *Right:* Samuel C. Johnson, born May 27, 1828, in Smaaland, Sweden, enlisted in Company C of the Fifteenth Wisconsin Infantry in 1861. The Fifteenth was known as the Scandinavian Regiment, and the men of Company C called themselves the Norway Bear Hunters. This photo is believed to have been taken in February 1862. A handwritten caption below the photo reads, "Co. C. Corporal Samuel C. Johnson (wounded Stones River, bullet through his thigh), D. Blair Wis. Spent 13 mo's in Southern Hospital and never regained his health."

WHi Image ID 69870 WHi Image ID 69875

Left: Carl Gustaf (Charles) Hammarqvist settled in Fort Atkinson and in 1860 became the first Swede elected to the Wisconsin legislature. *Right:* Second-generation Swedish American Irvine Luther Lenroot was born in Superior in 1869. He served as state assemblyman, U.S. representative, U.S. senator, and federal judge.

WHi Image ID 69876

Thure Kumlien had studied natural history before emigrating from Västergötland; he became an authority on Wisconsin's flora and fauna. From 1865 to 1870 he taught natural history at Albion Academy in Albion (Dane County), which became a pioneer institution in the study of ornithology. He is seen here at his work table in the Milwaukee Public Museum in 1887.

WHi Image ID 70110

Thure Kumlien arrived in the United States in 1843. He built this log house on his farm near Lake Koshkonong in 1847 and enlarged it in 1849.

WHi Image ID 69923

Swea Kumlien, daughter of Thure and Christina Kumlien, photographed in 1863 at age six. One of Kumlien's reasons for emigrating was his desire to marry Christina, who was a servant and who Kumlien's parents considered below their social class. Thure and Christina were married immediately upon their arrival in Wisconsin.

WHi Image ID 68551

The Swedish Ladies National Concerts, on their first American tour, appeared in Madison on August 27, 1889.

From K. S. Adlersparre, *Fredrika Bremer,*
Biografisk Studie, 1896, p. 128. Courtesy of the
Minnesota Historical Society, Neg. #88993

WHi Image ID 69925

Left: Fredrika Bremer, Swedish novelist and feminist, visited Wisconsin in 1850. Her lively letters to sister Agatha in Sweden chronicled her journey and reflected her impressions of the Wisconsin frontier. *Right:* Mrs. Bengt Petterson of the Swedish settlement at Pine Lake. Fredrika Bremer boarded with the "Widow Petterson" during her 1850 visit to Wisconsin; in her letters she described Mrs. Petterson as "a large woman, who in her youth must have been handsome . . . bent double and supported on a crutch-stick."

Courtesy of Orlin Anderson

The village school and its mainly Swedish student body, Stockholm, Pepin County, about 1892. Stockholm was one of the first Swedish settlements in western Wisconsin. Erik Petersson (1822–1887), a native of Värmland, founded the town in 1851.

WHi Image ID 69929

Main Street, Pepin, date unknown.

RELIGION

It is difficult to gauge the importance of religion in the lives of Swedish immigrants, partly because the statistics of nominal church membership reveal little about their personal spirituality. During the nineteenth century nearly the entire population of Sweden was baptized and confirmed in its state Lutheran Church. Increasingly after the 1850s, however, other denominations, most notably such Anglo-American ones as the Baptists, Methodists, and Seventh-day Adventists, attracted Swedes whose spiritual roads did not lead to the parishes of the Lutheran establishment.

Even in the state church many were dissatisfied with or alienated from formal religion. Long before the turn of the century it became common for Swedes to attend worship services only at Christmas and to mark significant events in their lives through religious ceremonies like baptism, confirmation, and marriage. There were more pious souls, as well, who were dissatisfied with the state church. They accepted Lutheran theology, but they found their parish pastors unsatisfactory or did not care to commune shoulder-to-shoulder with what they regarded as the unregenerate masses. Instead, they began to meet in private conventicles to study the Bible and, in some cases, to partake of the Lord's Supper without the presence of a clergyman.

When Swedes with these differing degrees and forms of religiosity emigrated, they found church membership to be a matter of personal choice in the United States. Accordingly, the official near-homogeneity of the Swedish religious landscape rapidly disintegrated among the immigrants to America. Many, almost certainly the majority, eschewed all formal affiliation with religious bodies. Others joined congregations representing a fairly wide spectrum of denominations. In 1860 Swedes helped organize the Augustana Synod, initially a combined Norwegian-Swedish denomination that continued those two national Lutheran traditions. A decade later, however, the Norwegians, along with a few Danes, formed their own synod of the same name. The Swedish congregations remained united and constituted the most direct American descendant of the state church of Sweden. In Trade Lake, Stockholm, West Sweden, Apple River, and nearly every other Wisconsin community with a sizeable number of Swedes, a Lutheran congregation was gathered and united with the Augustana Synod. By 1930 there were sixty-seven such units with a total membership of over five thousand, the largest being Superior.

Like Swedish immigrants in the United States as a whole, however, the overwhelming majority of those in Wisconsin did not join their birthright ethnic church. In 1930, when immigration from Scandinavia had been reduced to a trickle, Wisconsin had 18,808 Swedish-born residents, along with a second generation of 38,107 persons who had at least one Swedish-born parent. Despite its undeniable failure to attract a majority of the Swedes, the Augustana Synod continued to grow, and it spawned many educational and charitable institutions throughout the Midwest. In 1962 it merged with other Scandinavian and German Lutheran synods to form the Lutheran Church in America.

Other Swedes soon formed congregations affiliated with, and sometimes supported by, older Yankee denominations. Most numerous among these in Wisconsin were the Baptist churches. By 1930 there were twenty-three. They were smaller than their Lutheran rivals in most towns but were, at least according to their leaders, more vital. Many of these congregations are today part of the Baptist General Conference. Their pastors were originally trained with English-speaking Baptist seminarians in Chicago, but eventually the Swedish-Americans began their own educational program at what is now Bethel College and Theological Seminary near Saint Paul, Minnesota.

The third-largest distinctively Swedish denomination in Wisconsin is the Evangelical Covenant Church of America. It traces its roots to nineteenth-century pietist movements among the laity of the Swedish state church. After arriving in the United States, many pietists eschewed the Augustana Synod as too worldly, forming instead small congregations that eventually coalesced into the present denomination in 1885. It received financial and educational assistance from the Congregationalists until 1890 but, partly in resistance to that Yankee denomination's efforts to Americanize it, severed those ties that year and then opened North Park College in Chicago in 1891.

Smaller numbers of Swedes formed ethnic Methodist churches and, like the Baptists, enjoyed support from the parallel American denomination. Others joined Scandinavian Seventh-day Adventist bodies, the Evangelical Free Church, or several others, but in nearly all instances those churches fairly rapidly lost whatever Swedish flavor they once had.

There were simply not enough Swedes in them to make lasting imprints. Much the same can be said of the Swedish minorities in Wisconsin's far more numerous Norwegian Lutheran churches, where they could hear the Gospel preached and have the sacraments administered in a readily understandable if slightly foreign tongue.

Interdenominational relations seem to have been reasonably good among the state's Swedish immigrants. Like their Lutheran colleagues from the other Scandinavian countries and some areas of Germany, the Swedish Lutheran clergy initially resented the inroads that other faiths made in proselytizing Swedes who had been on the parish rolls of the established church in the old country. They soon accepted religious pluralism as a fact of life in the United States, however, and adapted to the voluntaryism that underlay church membership here. Representing what in the context of American Protestantism was a minority group, they had little choice. Marinette, for instance, boasted seven Scandinavian churches in 1890; four of them were Swedish, but only one of that quartet was Lutheran. The Trade Lake area also quickly became a Swedish-American microcosm of religious diversity. Rivalries existed among the denominations, but L. J. Ahlstrom, a Baptist minister, recalled late in life that "never did any strife or unfriendliness arise from divergent religious views to disturb the peaceful and friendly relations in the community."

Religious fragmentation may have accelerated the assimilation of Swedish immigrants into the mainstream of American society. The individual congregations were simply too small to remain bastions of Swedish culture. In and around Grantsburg in Burnett County, for instance, there were reportedly eleven Scandinavian churches at the beginning of the century. Several of them, however, numbered only a few dozen active members. This situation precluded establishment of effective parochial schools of the sort that immigrant church members of many nationalities and creeds organized, thus preserving their ethnic and religious heritage in the New World.

The English-speaking denominations that sponsored some immigrants' churches also contributed to the process of assimilation. Educational materials, for example, were readily available in English to serve the second generation. More willingly than their Lutheran counterparts, Swedish Baptist and other Protestant churches borrowed indigenous methods of raising funds, conducting revivals, and even preaching. Partly to meet competition from other denominations and counteract the indifference of many immigrants to Sweden's official religious forms, the Augustana Synod also adopted some of these ways but also retained much of its formal Old World Lutheran heritage. Religion thus served as agent of cultural retention as well as of assimilation among Swedish newcomers and their offspring.

ASSIMILATION AND THE IMMIGRANT PRESS

The rate at which various ethnic groups assimilated in the United States has long been a matter of interest (and occasional controversy) among historians. When northern European immigration was at or near its peak — from the 1880s until the 1920s — some nationalistic Americans argued that the Scandinavians more readily adapted to the culture of the New World than did immigrants from southern and eastern Europe. While it is difficult to measure assimilation, there is considerable evidence that in Wisconsin Swedish ways generally yielded soon to those of the more dominant, English-speaking Yankee stock.

One of the first institutions to lose ground was the homogeneous Swedish family. Unmarried men outnumbered single women from Sweden, and many of these pioneers simply remained bachelors. "Eligible women are as rare here as blizzards on Midsummer Night's Eve," wrote a dejected newcomer in Marinette in 1897. "The few Swedish girls who come marry almost immediately. They usually choose the men with the most gray whiskers in their beards." Swedes who wished to take wives often turned to Germans, Norwegians, or other immigrants in search of brides or, of course, to the native Yankee population.

The rate of Swedish intermarriage was higher than for Germans and Norwegians, but not as high as the Danish level. The second generation naturally included many people with only one Swedish parent. Raised in homes where that language was seldom used, they hardly could have had strong feelings of ethnic identity. Some parents commented on the Americanization of their children with regret and sought to endow them with at least a rudimentary knowledge of Swedish; others accepted the cultural transition as inevitable; a few welcomed it. Practically no effort was made outside the churches to retain Swedish or encourage bilingualism in institutions. Apart from a few isolated communities, the number of Swedes in Wisconsin simply did not make it feasible.

The immigrant press helped many ethnic groups uphold their identity in the United States, and that of the Swedes was no exception. Beginning in the 1850s, several hundred Swedish-American newspapers,
most of them short-lived, rolled from the presses to enlighten newcomers
in communities from New England to Puget Sound. A few remain, the
largest being *Svenska Amerikanaren Tribunen* (Swedish-American Tribune)
of Chicago. Swedish journalists in Wisconsin made a relatively modest
contribution to this output. The *Wisconsin Svenska Tribunen* first appeared in Superior in 1883 but eventually moved to Minneapolis. Another newspaper that left Wisconsin was *Marinette Tribunen*, until 1909
appropriately titled *Förposten* (Outpost). In 1917 its editor, G. L. Forsen,
sold it to *Medborgaren* (Compatriot) of Escanaba, Michigan. Historians
agree that World War I dealt ethnicity many telling blows, of which the
fate of the Swedish press is but one example. Before their demise, however, these newspapers conveyed fairly up-to-date national and regional
news as well as reports from Sweden. They could not compete with the
Chicago-based Swedish papers' far greater resources, however. Immigrants throughout much of the United States subscribed to these, and in
heavily Swedish Burnett and Polk Counties, the English-language press
reigned. "Our newspaper was in English," conceded L. J. Ahlstrom,
"but its regular readership consisted almost exclusively of Scandinavians." Weekly exposure to the language and thinking of small-town
Yankee editors helped to forge the immigrant mind, shaping it to con-
form at least partly to that of middle America.

The availability of English-language newspapers in most Wisconsin
communities, and the lack of Swedish ones, helped stimulate immigrants' transition to the vernacular, but other factors undoubtedly
played larger roles in fostering use of English. For thousands of newcomers, the change began upon their arrival in the United States when
immigration officials anglicized their foreign surnames. Many a Nilsson,
for instance, left Castle Garden or Ellis Island in New York with papers
giving their names as Nelson. Haakonsson frequently became Hawkins
and Johansson Johnson. Others voluntarily changed at least the foreign
orthography of their names: Ahlströnm, for example, invariably became
Åhlstrom, while Ångström was simplified to Engstrom. Common
patronymics such as Olsson, Hansson, and Carlsson lost an "s" in most
cases, bringing them into line with analogous English names such as
Jackson and Wilson. The Friman clan that gained some prominence
among the earliest Swedes in Wisconsin during the 1840s soon became

Freeman. Scandinavian consonants also caused difficulties. After settling in Trempealeau, pugnacious Kalle Kjlman gave up correcting Yankees who butchered both his names and "voluntarily" became Charlie Kellman. Swedish-American history abounds with accounts of similar compromises.

The second generation completed this linguistic transition. Educated in English-language schools (even in the few predominantly Swedish areas) and surrounded by children of newcomers from Germany, Norway, the British Isles, and other countries as well as migrants from other parts of the United States, most children of Swedish immigrants had little opportunity to use or even hear their parents' tongue outside the home and, in some instances, the church. Nor do most seem to have shown much desire to. The Lutheran Augustana Synod sought vigorously to retain its members' children, but equivocation on the language issue militated against the goal. As early as 1872 its president conceded that "the language question is becoming a difficult one in our church work, and those difficulties are already beginning in many places, especially in the cities where they are quite serious with respect to the Sunday schools." He lamented that Swedish-American children without a conversational command of their parents' tongue were drifting toward the congregations of "American" (i.e., non-Lutheran) denominations. During the 1880s the Augustana Synod began to organize English-language churches that also attracted non-Swedes, and during the following decade English became the medium of instruction at the Synod's Gustavus Adolphus College in Saint Peter, Minnesota. A survey of its congregations in 1908 indicated that about 47 percent of the children confirmed that year were confirmed in English.

The impact of World War I nearly completed the Swedish immigrants' linguistic transition both in Wisconsin and the United States as a whole. After President Woodrow Wilson reversed his noninterventionist policy in 1917 and American doughboys embarked for France, xenophobic hysteria led to curtailing the use of foreign languages. Wisconsin's large immigrant population did not have to endure a ban on their European tongues as did, for instance, their counterparts in Iowa. But many, even non-Germans, suffered some degree of social ostracism. "We never speak Swedish on the street," wrote a Swede from Ashland near the end of the war. "Olof [a brother of the writer] was roughed up by some of the Yankee boys in a restaurant last week."

POLITICS

Politics also played a role in the process of Americanization. Constitutional democracy had evolved at a moderate pace in Sweden during the nineteenth century, so many Swedes already had some practical experience in popular government. Swedish-Americans quickly took advantage of their modest previous experience and their new land's generous suffrage, becoming active participants in American government on several levels. Voting privileges were easily acquired in most states, as in Wisconsin, where resident male aliens merely had to declare their intentions to become citizens in order to be enfranchised. Like other midwestern Scandinavians, the state's Swedes tended to support the Republican Party until the watershed decade of the 1890s. Their political leanings helped them win both social and political acceptance by the middle-class, Protestant majority in the party — a welcome that long eluded newcomers from Italy, Ireland, Germany, and eastern Europe, who were often regarded as unthinking pawns of Democratic machine politics.

Whatever consensus may have existed among Scandinavian Americans dissolved near the end of the century, though, as the depression of 1893 nurtured disillusionment with conservatism. Populism and progressivism arose as alternatives. Many Swedes, however, openly eschewed partisanship altogether and ran as independents for all manner of local office, particularly in the rural areas of northwestern Wisconsin. There they held township and county positions for decades and in some areas were sufficiently dominant to conduct the affairs of government in Swedish.

No immigrant from Sweden gained prominence in Wisconsin state politics. But Irvine Lenroot, a second-generation Swedish American, rose to the upper legislative echelons in both Madison and Washington. His father, born in southern Sweden in 1832 and baptized Lars Larsson, changed his all-too-common surname to Linderoth before arriving in Boston in 1854. Anglicizing the spelling to Lenroot, he and his Swedish immigrant bride temporarily occupied a farm in the wilds of Polk County before moving to Superior in 1857. Irvine, named after a local Yankee schoolteacher, was born there twelve years later.

Trained at a business college in Duluth as a stenographer, Irvine

Lenroot worked initially as a law clerk and court reporter but, after several years of self-tutelage, was admitted to the bar in 1898. In the meantime, he had become involved in progressive Republican politics and was elected to the state assembly in 1900, the same year that voters sent fellow progressive Robert M. La Follette to the governor's mansion. In 1908 Lenroot began a ten-year stint in the House of Representatives, where he and other insurgent Republicans challenged their party's commitment to high tariffs and other conservative doctrines. Unlike many other Progressives, however, Lenroot supported military conscription and American intervention in World War I. In 1918 he was elected to fill a vacant seat in the Senate, and two years later voters returned him for a full six-year term. After the war Senator Lenroot campaigned for United States membership in the League of Nations. His stand on this bitter issue may have contributed to the Republican Party's final choice of the conservative Calvin Coolidge as Warren G. Harding's running mate in the presidential election of 1920. Lenroot's meteoric rise as a legislator ended abruptly when he was defeated for renomination in 1926, and he finished his career as a federal judge in New York City.

Swedish immigration enjoyed a moderate upswing during the early 1920s. Wisconsin, however, received few of these newcomers. Its number of Swedish-born residents declined from 26,196 in 1900 to 18,808 thirty years later as old age and natural attrition took their toll. This, together with assimilation, eroded the explicitly Swedish presence in the state. The tiny number of Swedes who have come to Wisconsin since World War II generally have been businesspeople, academicians, and other privileged people who have little in common with the trailblazers of the earlier era.

The percentage of Wisconsinites born in Sweden never has been large, and in the twentieth century the state never has ranked among the top half-dozen in attracting Swedes. How can this be explained, given Wisconsin's reputation as one of the leading Scandinavian settlement areas and the prominence of Danes and especially Norwegians in the state's history? Part of the answer lies in the time frame of Swedish emigration and the availability of cheap land in Wisconsin. As early as 1841, Carl Johan Friman wrote home from the Town of Salem in modern Kenosha County and urged Swedes "to come soon, because the land is rapidly being settled, largely by Norwegians." Very few Swedes, however, heard this advice or heeded it during the next quarter-century. In the meantime, Irish, Norwegian, German, and other immigrants had acquired most of the productive acreages in southern and central Wisconsin. Land-hungry Swedes were compelled to look farther west to Minnesota, Kansas, Nebraska, and elsewhere.

The Swedish settlements in northern Wisconsin played minor parts in this historic pageant of westward migration. The states to the west and southwest still could offer cheap farms and, in many cases, free homesteads during the 1880s when Swedish immigration reached its zenith. In this respect, Wisconsin could no longer compete effectively, despite limited official efforts to attract northern Europeans. Moreover, Minnesota's Board of Immigration enjoyed superior funding and boldly stationed agents in Milwaukee and Chicago to greet newcomers as they stepped ashore. Consequently, many Swedes remained in Wisconsin only for the few hours it took them to travel by rail to the Minnesota border. Of the more than twenty-five thousand who disembarked in Milwaukee from 1879 through 1884, fewer then eight thousand settled in the Badger State. Industrial employment attracted others to Chicago, but again Wisconsin could not compete on an even footing, even when its factory towns along Lake Michigan began to burgeon. Owing chiefly to these factors, Wisconsin, whose Swedes never comprised even 2 percent of its entire population, ended up being sandwiched between heavily Swedish northern Illinois and eastern Minnesota.

If newcomers from Scotland and England were the "invisible immigrants" of nineteenth- and early twentieth-century America, as some historians have called them, then those from Sweden might well be termed the transparent Scandinavians of Wisconsin. Probably none of the state's other ethnic groups from continental Europe so quickly became nearly indistinguishable from its Yankee stock as did her Swedes, and surely none was more readily accepted by the Yankees. In appearance these settlers were decidedly Nordic, in faith they were nominally and in many cases authentically Protestant, and in politics they maintained a low profile. Few made a determined effort to preserve their distinctly Swedish heritage; indeed, their geographical distribution rendered such a step nearly impossible. Within a generation, the Swedes had become a modest and inseparable part of the ethnic landscape of rural Wisconsin.

WHi Image ID 69930

Getting in the livestock, probably near Stockholm, Pepin County, c. 1910. Most of Stockholm's early settlers came in 1853–1854 from Karlskoga in Värmland. In 1854 155 of 280 emigrants died on the treacherous trek to Stockholm.

Albert Peterson Collection, Burnett County Historical Society

The cook shack and bunkhouse on the Albert Peterson farm at Trade Lake, c. 1910. Shown are Albin Lindquist, Adolph Lindquist, Joel Bratley, Ed Bratley, Albert Anderson, Gilbert Swanberg, Herbert Burch, Charles Peterson, and Albert Peterson.

Peterson family portrait. Adolph Peterson (seated, left) emigrated to the United States from Norike, Sweden, with his parents in 1881. Their fare was paid to Rush City, Minnesota, and they walked from there to the Trade River area in Burnett County, where they settled. Albert Peterson (standing, right) lived on the family's Trade Lake farm all his life.

Albert Peterson Collection, Burnett County Historical Society

Young Burnett County Swedes dressed in summer finery to celebrate the 4th of July, 1916. From left: Esther Larson, Hilive Peterson, Albert Peterson, Agnes Brask, Hilma Brask, Raymond Peterson, Charley Brask, Amanda Brask, and Helen Larson. Albert Peterson and Helen Larson were married two weeks later, on July 16.

Albert Peterson Collection, Burnett County Historical Society

Wedding of Olga Lundeen and Oscar Lystad at the Erick Lundeen home, Trade Lake, 1915. Everyone in the picture is Swedish, and most were probably conversant in their home language, which persisted here well into the 1920s.

WHi Image ID 69932

The Wallin brothers' threshing rig near Stockholm, Pepin County, c. 1915.

WHi Image ID 69934

Village school, Stockholm, Pepin County, c. 1910. The teacher, Amy Larson (standing, far right), was the niece twice-removed of Erik Petersson, who founded the town.

WHi Image ID 69936

Rural mail carrier, Stockholm. In summertime the same boxlike rig was mounted on wheels.

WHi Image ID 69939

The family of Frank Wilson — who was named Frank Josephson in his Swedish homeland — on the porch of their Pepin County home, c. 1910.

Albert Peterson Collection, Burnett County Historical Society

A summer afternoon at the John P. Larson homestead in Burnett County, date unknown. The women pictured, all Swedes, are Helen (Larson) Peterson (second from
left) and her sister, Anna Larson (third from left), two of their Larson cousins, and
young Arlene Peterson.

Albert Peterson Collection, Burnett County Historical Society

Helen (Larson) Peterson and baby Arlene set out on the two-mile buggy ride to visit
grandparents.

Albert Peterson Collection, Burnett County Historical Society

Frank Larson plowing with Ned and Nellie on the Albert Peterson farm near Trade Lake, Burnett County, 1921.

Albert Peterson Collection, Burnett County Historical Society

Sawing an immense elm tree into lumber on the Gotfred Eckberg farm, Trade Lake, Burnett County, 1927. The Fallstrom brothers, Harry and Emil, moved their steam-powered sawmill to the site for several weeks to work on the project.

WHi Image ID 69940

Alfresco portrait at the Erick Hattstrom home, Stockholm vicinity, Pepin County, date unknown.

Courtesy of R. G. Arveson

In August 1951, residents of Frederic (Polk County) celebrated the village's Golden Jubilee — the fiftieth anniversary of its founding in 1901. Many attendees wore traditional Scandinavian dress. Approximately seventy percent of the village's settlers were of Swedish descent.

THE WRITINGS OF FREDRIKA BREMER, 1850

Fredrika Bremer, a forty-nine-year-old Swedish novelist and feminist, visited Wisconsin in late September and early October of 1850. Her two-week trek through the southern section of the state was part of an American tour in which she met many literary and political figures. Bremer was already well known in the United States because of popular English-language editions of her novels. While in America, she wrote detailed letters to her sister, Agatha, which later were published in Europe. An English-language translation of this travel account appeared in 1856 under the title Homes of the New World.

The excerpts printed below chronicle her trip from Milwaukee to Galena, Illinois, on a "diligence," or public stagecoach. Her account includes a detailed description of life among a settlement of Swedes at Pine Lake in Waukesha County as well as her observations about Watertown, Milwaukee, Madison, Koshkonong, and Blue Mounds. The resulting text offers insights about both the experiences of Swedish immigrants in Wisconsin and how early Wisconsin appeared to a Swedish visitor. The text printed here is taken from George C. Brown, ed., "A Swedish Traveler in Early Wisconsin: The Observations of Fredrika Bremer," Wisconsin Magazine of History, 61 (1977–78): 300–318; 62 (1978–79): 41–56.

Watertown, October First

Watertown is a little, newly sprung-up, infant town of two thousand inhabitants. The small, neat houses, most of them of wood and painted white, and very smart and clean, were scattered upon the green slopes between the wood and the river. . . . The further I advance into the West, the more clear it becomes to me that . . . people in the great West are as yet principally occupied in the acquisition of the material portion of life, in a word, by "business!" People have not as yet time to turn themselves to the sun.

But the churches, the schools, and the asylums which are in progress of erection, and those small houses and homes which are beginning to adorn themselves with flowers, to surround themselves with gardens — they prove that the light-life is struggling into being. . . .

I wrote to you last from Chicago. From Chicago I went by steamer across Lake Michigan to Milwaukee, escorted by a pleasant and warm-hearted young man, Mr. R. The proprietor of the steamer would not allow me to pay for my passage. The voyage was sunbright and excellent. We lay to at small infant towns on the shore, such as Southbord [Southport; now Kenosha], Elgin, Racine, all having sprung up within the last seven or eight years, and in a fair way of growing great under the influence of trade and the navigation of the Lake.

I was met at Milwaukee by Herr L[ange], a Swedish gentleman resident there as a merchant, who had invited me to his house, and who now conducted me thither, where I was most kindly received i. his wife, a little, good-tempered Irish lady. That was in the evening. The next morning was rainy, but afterward cleared up, and became one of the most lovely days. The whole of the forenoon I was obliged to enact the lioness to an incessant stream of callers, ladies and gentlemen, received from them presents of flowers, books, verses, and through all was obliged to be polite, answer the same questions over and over again, and play over and over again on the piano the same ballads and polkas. Some of these people were evidently interesting people, from whose conversation I could have derived pleasure and profit; but ah! This stream carries all pearls along with it.

I was this forenoon in a large ladies' school, where I saw many handsome young girls, made them a speech, and congratulated them on being Americans; I also saw some agreeable teachers, and then, again, more gentlemen and ladies. An important reformation in female schools is taking place in these Western states at the present time under the guidance of a Miss Beecher, sister to the highly-gifted young minister at Brooklyn, and who is a kind of lady-abbess in educational matters. In the afternoon I was driven about to see all the lions of the place in a carriage, which a gentleman of the town had placed at my disposal. It was very agreeable, for the town is beautiful — has a charming situation on elevated ground, between Lake Michigan and Milwaukee River, and increases with all its might. Four great school-houses, one in each quarter of the town, shone in the sunlight with their ascending cupolas. They are as yet in progress of erection, are all alike, and in a good style of architecture — ornamental without pomp. I saw some handsome, well-built streets, with handsome shops and houses, quite different to those of Chicago.

Nearly all the houses in Milwaukee are built of brick, a peculiar kind of brick, which is made here from the clay of the neighborhood, and which makes a brick of a pale yellow color, which gives the city a very cheerful appearance, as if the sun were always shining there. I saw also lovely country houses in the outskirts, with splendid and extensive prospects over lake and land. Milwaukee, not Chicago, deserves to be called "Queen of the Lake." She stands a splendid city on those sunny heights, and grows and extends herself every day. Nearly half of the inhabitants are Germans, and they occupy a portion of the city to themselves, which is called "German Town." This lies on the other side of the River Milwaukee. Here one sees German houses, German inscriptions over the doors or signs, German physiognomies. Here are published German newspapers; and many Germans live here who never learn English, and seldom go beyond the German town.

AMONG THE SWEDES AT PINE LAKE

On the morning of the 29th of September I arrived at this, the first Swedish colony of the West. Herr Lange drove me there in a little carriage, along a road which was any thing but good, through a solitary region, a distance of somewhat above twenty miles from Milwaukee. It was on a Sunday morning, a beautiful sunshiny day.

There remain still of the little Swedish colony of Pine Lake about half a dozen families, who live as farmers in the neighborhood. It is lake scenery, and as lovely and romantic as any may be imagined — regular Swedish lake scenery; and one can understand how those first Swedish emigrants were enchanted, so that, without first examining the quality of the soil, they determined to found here a New Sweden, and to build a New Upsala! I spent the forenoon in visiting the various Swedish families. Nearly all live in log-houses, and seem to be in somewhat low circumstances. The most prosperous seemed to be that of the smith; he, I fancy, had been a smith in Sweden, and had built himself a pretty frame house in the forest; he was a really good fellow, and had a nice young Norwegian for his wife: also a Mr. Bergman [also referred to as Bergvall], who had been a gentleman in Sweden, but who was here a clever, hard-working peasant farmer; had some acres of good land, which he cultivated ably, and was getting on well.

He was of a remarkably cheerful, good-tempered, and vigorous Swedish temperament; he had fine cattle, which he himself attended to, and a good harvest of maize, which now stood cut in the field to dry in the sun. He had enlarged his log-house by a little frame-house which he had built up to it; and in the log-house he had the very prettiest, kindest, most charming young Swedish wife, with cheeks as fresh as red roses, such as one seldom sees in America, and that spite of her having a four-weeks' old little boy, her first child, and having, with the assistance only of her young sister, to do all the work of the house herself. It was a joyous and happy home, a good Swedish home, in the midst of an American wilderness. And the dinner which I had there was, with all its simplicity, exquisitely good, better than many a one which I have eaten in the great and magnificent hotels of America. We were ten Swedes at dinner; most of the number young men, one of whom was betrothed to the handsome young sister of the mistress of the house. Good milk, excellent bread and butter, the most savory water-fowl and delicious tarts, cordial hospitality, cheerfulness and good feeling, crowning the board; and, besides all the rest, that beautiful Swedish language spoken by every one — these altogether made that meal a regular festival to me.

Our young and handsome hostess attended to the table, sometimes went out into the kitchen — the adjoining room — to look after the cooking, or to attend to her little baby in the cradle, which cried aloud for its dinner, then came back again to us, and still the roses bloomed freshly on her cheeks, and still the kind smile was on her lips, spite of an anxious look in those clear blue eyes. Both sisters were blonde, with round countenances, blue eyes, light hair, fair complexions, regular white teeth, lovely and slender figures — true Swedes, especially the young wife, a lovely specimen of the young Swedish woman.

In the afternoon she took me by a little path through the wood, down to the wonderfully beautiful Pine Lake, on the banks of which, but deeper still in the woods, her home was situated, and near to which the other Swedish houses also stood. On our way I asked her about her life, and thus came to hear, but without the least complaint on her part, of its many difficulties.

The difficulty of obtaining the help of servants, male and female, is one of the inconveniences and difficulties which the colonists of the West have to encounter. They must either pay for labor at an enormously high rate — and often it is not to be had on any terms — or they must do without it; and if their own powers of labor fail, either through sickness or any other misfortune, then is want the inevitable consequence. There is need of much affection and firm reliance for any one, under such circumstances, to venture on settling down here; but these both lived in the heart of the young Swede, and her eyes sparkled as she spoke of her husband, his kind, good heart, and his vigor both of mind and body. While we were standing beside that quiet lake, garlanded by thick branching trees and underwood, splendid with the coloring of autumn, we heard the husband's voice as he drove the oxen down to water, and soon we saw their huge horns pushing a way through the thick foliage. Our cheerful, well-bred host was now a brisk ox-driver.

After this we betook ourselves to the oldest house of the colony on Pine Lake, where lived Mrs. Bergvall's mother, the Widow Petterson, and who expected us to coffee; and thither we drove, Mr. Lange and I, in our little open carriage, the other Swedish families driving there also, but with oxen. A young Swede, who had married a fat, elderly American widow, was of the company. I saw them going on through the wood, she sitting with her parasol on the carriage, while her young husband drove the oxen. One of Mrs. Petterson's sons, a young man of about twenty, rode before us as a guide through the labyrinths of the wood. Thus we arrived at a log-house, resembling one of the peasant cottages around Aersta, standing upon a green hill, commanding the most beautiful view over the lake, which was here seen in nearly its whole extent.

Mrs. Petterson, a large woman, who in her youth must have been handsome, came out to receive me, bent double and supported on a crutch-stick, but her open countenance beaming with kindness. She is not yet fifty, but is aged and broken down before her time by severe labor and trouble. I saw in her a true type of the Swedish woman of the middle class, with that overflowing heart which finds vent in tears, in kind looks and words, and who does not measure by any niggard rule either what the hand gives or the tongue speaks; a regularly magnificent, warm-hearted gossip, who loves to entertain her friends with good cheer as much as she loves her life. She regaled us with the most delicious coffee, and flavored that warm beverage with warm, kind looks and words.

Her husband began here as a farmer, but neither he nor his wife were accustomed to hard work; their land was poor (with the exception of Bergvall's farm, all the land around Pine Lake appears to be of a poor quality), they could not get help, and they were without the conveniences of life; they had a large family, which kept increasing; they endured incredible hardships. Mrs. Petterson, while suckling her children, was compelled to do the most laborious work; bent double with rheumatism, she was often obliged to wash for the whole family on her knees.

Her husband was at last obliged to give up farming; he then took to shoemaking, and at this trade succeeded in making a livelihood for himself and his family. He had now been dead a few years, and his widow was preparing to leave the little house and garden, which she could no longer look after, and remove to her son-in-law Bergvall's.

She felt herself worn out, old, and finished before her time, as she said; but still did not regret having come to America, because, as regarded her children and their future, she saw a new world opened to them, richer and happier than that which the mother country could have offered them, and she would have been glad to have purchased this future for them at the sacrifice of her own life; she would be well contented to go down to the grave, even before her time, and there to have done with her crutch. Their children, four sons and four daughters — the two youngest born here, and still children — were all of them agreeable, and some of them remarkably handsome, in particular the two youngest boys — Knut and Sten. Sten rowed me in a little boat along the shores of the charming lake; he was a beautiful, slender youth of seventeen; and as he sat there in his white shirt-sleeves, with his blue silk waistcoat, with his clear, dark-blue eyes, and a pure, good expression in that lovely, fresh youthful countenance, he was the perfect idea of a shepherd in some beautiful idyll. The sisters, when we were alone, praised Knut and Sten as sincerely kind and good lads, who would do any thing for their sisters and their home.

We rowed along the wooded shores, which, brilliant in their autumnal coloring, were reflected in the mirror-like waters. And here, upon a lofty promontory covered with splendid masses of wood, was New Upsala to stand — such was the intention of Unonius and his friends when they first came to this wild region, and were enchanted with its beauty. Ah! That wild district will not maintain Upsala's sons. I saw the desolate houses where he, Unonius, and Schneidau struggled in vain to live. . . .

Returning to the log-house, we spent the evening — one-and-twenty Swedes altogether — in games, songs, and dancing, exactly as if in Sweden. I had, during the whole time of my journey to the West, been conning over in my mind a speech which I would make to my countrymen in the West; I thought how I would bear to them a salutation from their mother country, and exhort them to create a new Sweden in that new land! I thought that I would remind them of all that the Old Country had of great and beautiful, in memory, in thought, in man-

ners and customs; I wished to awaken in their souls the inspiration of a
New Scandinavia. I had often myself been deeply affected by the
thoughts and the words which I intended to make use of.

But now, when I was at the very place where I longed to be, and
thought about my speech, I could not make it. Nor did I make it at all. I
felt myself happy in being with my countrymen, happy to find them so
agreeable and so Swedish still in the midst of a foreign land. But I felt
more disposed for merriment than solemnity. I therefore, instead of
making my speech, read to the company that little story by Hans Christian Andersen called "The Pine-tree," and then incited my countrymen
to sing Swedish songs. Neither were those beautiful Swedish voices lost
here in the New World, and I was both affected and impressed with a
deep solemnity when the men, led by Bergvall, sang, with their fresh,
clear voices, "Up, Swedes! for king and fatherland," and after that many
other old national songs. Swedish hospitality, cheerfulness, and song live
here as vigorously as ever they did in the Old Country.

The old lady, Petterson, had got ready a capital entertainment; incomparably excellent coffee, and tea especially; good venison, fruit,
tarts, and many good things, all as nicely and as delicately set out as if on
a prince's table. The young sons of the house waited upon us. At home,
in Sweden, it would have been the daughters. All were cordial and joyous. When the meal was over we had again songs, and after that dancing. . . . We then parted with cordial shaking of hands and mutual good
wishes, and all and each returned to their homes in the star-bright night.

I was to remain at Mrs. Petterson's, but not without some uneasiness
on my part as to the prospect of rest; for, however sumptuous had been
the entertainment of the evening, yet still the state of the house testified
of the greatest lack of the common conveniences of life; and I had to
sleep in the sister's bed with Mrs. Petterson, and six children and grand-
children lay in the adjoining room, which was the kitchen.

Among these was young Mrs. Bergvall, with her little baby and her
little step-son; for, when she was about to return home with Herr Lange,
his horses became frightened by the pitch darkness of the night and
would not go on, and she herself becoming frightened too, would not
venture with her little children. Bergvall, therefore, set off alone through
the forest, and I heard his wife calling after him: "Dear Bergvall, mind
and milk the white cow well again to-night." (It is the men in this country who milk the cows, as well as attend to all kinds of out-of-door busi-

ness.) He replied to her with a cheerful "Yes." And Mrs. Bergvall and her mother prayed me to excuse there being so many of them in the house that night, &c.-me, the stranger, and who was the cause of this throng! It was I who ought to have asked for excuse; and I would rather have slept outside the house than not have appeared satisfied and pleased with every thing within it. And when Mrs. Petterson had lain down, she said, "Ah, Miss Bremer, how much more people can bear than can be believed possible!"

I sighed, and said, "Yes, indeed!" gave up the search for an extinguisher, which could not be found, put out the candle, therefore, with a piece of paper, and crept into my portion of the bed, where, though my sleep was nothing to speak of, I yet rested comfortably. I was glad the next morning to feel well, and to rise with the sun, which, however, shone somewhat dimly through the mist above the beautiful lake. It was a cool, moist morning; but these warm-hearted people, the warm and good coffee, and the hospitable entertainment, warmed both soul and body.

It was with heartfelt emotion and gratitude that I, after breakfast, took leave of my Swedish friends. Mrs. Petterson would have given me the only valuable which she now possessed — a great, big gold ring; but I could not consent to it. How richly had she gifted me already! We parted, not without tears. That amiable young mother, her cheeks blooming like wild roses, accompanied me through the wood, walking beside the carriage silently and kindly, and silently we parted with a cordial pressure of the hand and a glance. That lovely young Swede was the most beautiful flower of that American wilderness. She will beautify and ennoble it.

Heartfelt kindness and hospitality, seriousness and mirth in pure family life — these characteristics of Swedish life, where it is good — should be transplanted into the Western wilderness by the Swedish colonists, as they are in this instance. That day among the Swedes by Pine Lake; that splendid old lady; those handsome, warm-hearted men; those lovely, modest, and kind young women; that affectionate domestic life; that rich hospitality in poor cottagers — all are to me a pledge of it. The Swedes must continue to be Swedes, even in the New World; and their national life and temperament, their dances and games, their star-songs and hymns, must give to the western land a new element of life and beauty. They must continue to be such a people in this country that earnestness and mirth may prosper among them, and that they may be pious and joyful at the same time, as well on Sundays as on all other days. And they must learn from the American people that regularity and perseverance, that systematizing in life, in which they are yet deficient. A new Scandinavia shall one day bloom in the valley of the Mississippi in the great assembly of peoples there, with men and women, games, and songs, and dances. . . .

During this day I put some questions to all the Swedes whom I met regarding the circumstances and the prospects of the Swedes in this new country, as compared with those of the old, and their answers were very nearly similar, and might be comprised in the following:

"If we were to work as hard in Sweden as we do here, we should be as well off there, and often better.

"None who are not accustomed to hard, agricultural labor ought to become farmers in this country.

"No one who is in any other way well off in his native land ought to come hither, unless, having a large family, he may do so on account of his children; because children have a better prospect here for their future than at home. They are admitted into schools for nothing; receive good education, and easily have an opportunity of maintaining themselves.

"But the old, who are not accustomed to hard labor, and the absence of all conveniences of life, can not long resist the effects of the climate, sickness, and other hardships.

"Young unmarried people may come hither advantageously, if they will begin by taking service with others. As servants in American families they will be well fed and clothed, and have good wages, so that they may soon lay by a good deal. For young and healthy people it is not difficult to get on well here; but they must be prepared to work really hard, and in the beginning to suffer from the climate and from the diseases prevalent in this country.

"The Norwegians get on better in a general way than the Swedes, because they apply themselves more to work and housewifery, and think less of amusement than we do. They also emigrate in larger companies, and thus can help one another in their work and settling down."

The same evening that I spent at Mrs. Petterson's, I saw a peasant from Norrland, who had come with his son to look at her little farm, having some thought of purchasing it. He had lately come hither from Sweden, but merely, as he said, to look about him. He was, however, so well pleased with what he saw, that he was going back to fetch his wife, his children, and his movables, and then return here to settle. The man was one of the most beautiful specimens of the Swedish peasant, tall, strong-limbed, with fine, regular features, large, dark blue eyes, his hair parted above his forehead, and falling straight down both sides of his face — a strong, honest, good, and noble countenance, such as it does one good to look upon. The son was quite young, but promised to resemble his father in manly beauty. It grieved me to think that such men should leave Sweden. Yet the new Sweden will be all the better for them.

With that ascending September sun, Mr. Lange and I advanced along the winding paths of the wood till we reached the great high road, where we were to meet the diligence [public stagecoach] by which I was to proceed to Madison, while Mr. Lange returned to Milwaukee. Many incomparably lovely lakes, with romantic shores, are scattered through this district, and human habitations are springing up along them daily. I heard the names of some of these lakes — Silver Lake, Nobbmaddin Lake, as well as Lake Naschota, a most beautiful lake, on the borders of which I awaited the diligence. Here stood a beautiful newly-built country house, the grounds of which were beginning to be laid out. Openings had been made here and there in the thick wild forest, to give fine views of that romantic lake.

The diligence came. It was full of gentlemen; but they made room. I squeezed myself in among the strangers, and, supported by both hands upon my umbrella, as by a stick, I was shaken, or rather hurled, unmercifully hither and thither upon the new-born roads of Wisconsin, which are no roads at all, but a succession of hills, and holes, and waterpools, in which first one wheel sank, and then the other, while the opposite one stood high up in the air. Sometimes the carriage came to a sudden stand-still, half overturned in a hole, and it was some time before it could be dragged out again, only to be thrown into the same position on the other side.

To me that mode of traveling seemed really incredible, nor could I comprehend how, at that rate, we should ever get along at all. Sometimes we drove for a considerable distance in the water, so deep that I expected to see the whole equipage either swim or sink altogether. And when we reached dry land, it was only to take the most extraordinary leaps over stocks and stones. They comforted me by telling me that the diligence was not in the habit of being upset very often! And, to my astonishment, I really did arrive at Watertown without being overturned, but was not able to proceed without a night's rest.

Madison, October Fifth

I proceed with my letter in the capital of Wisconsin, a pretty little town (mostly consisting of villas and gardens) most beautifully situated between four lakes, the shores of which are fringed with live-oaks. I am here in a good and handsome house on the shore of one of the lakes, surrounded by all the comforts of life, and among kind, cultivated people and friends. At Watertown I discovered that the Public Conveyance Company had given orders that I was to have free transit through all parts of the state, and the host of the hotel, where every thing was very good and excellent, would not be paid for my entertainment there, but thanked me for "my call at his house." That one may term politeness!

At Watertown I became acquainted with some Danes who resided there, and spent a pleasant evening with one of them, just married to a young and charming Norwegian lady. They were comfortable, and seemed to be doing well in the city, where he was engaged in trade. An elderly Danish gentleman, however, who also was in trade in the city, did not seem to get on so well, but complained of the want of society and of some cheerful amusement in the long and solitary evenings. He was a widower, and widowers, or indeed men without wives and domestic life in America, lead solitary lives, particularly in small towns and in the country.

I left that kind little city with regret, in order to be shook onward to Madison. My portmanteau had been sent on by mistake from Watertown, by some diligence, I knew not how or whither, but thanks to the electric telegraphs, which sent telegraphic messages in three directions, I received again the next day my lost effects safe and sound. It is remarkable that in all directions throughout this young country, along these rough roads, which are no roads at all, run these electric wires from tree to tree, from post to post, along the prairie-land, and bring towns and villages into communication.

The road to Madison was difficult, but having a greater resemblance to a road than that between Milwaukee and Watertown. There were but few passengers in the diligence, and I was able, therefore, to place myself a little more comfortably; a bright Aurora Borealis shone across the prairie-land as we drove along in that starlight night, and the glow-worms glimmered in the grass which bordered the road. The journey was not unpleasant. The vast, solitary, verdant, billowy extent, embraced by the vast, star-lit firmament, had in it something grand and calm. I sat silent and quiet. At half past eleven I reached Madison, where it was with difficulty that room could be found for me at the inn, or that any body would take charge of me. The next day, however, I found both house, and home, and friends, and every thing was excellent. . . .

I had heard speak of a flourishing Norwegian settlement, in a district called Kos[h]konong, about twenty miles from Madison, and having expressed a wish to visit it, a kind young lady, Mrs. C., offered to drive me there with her carriage and horses.

The next day we set off in a little open carriage, with a Norwegian lad as driver. The weather was mild and sunny, and the carriage rolled lightly along the country, which is here hilly, and, having a solid surface, makes naturally good roads. The whole of the first part of the way lay through new and mostly wild, uncultivated land, but which every where resembled an English park, with grassy hills and dales, the grass waving tall and yellow, and scattered with oak wood. The trees were not lofty, and the green sward under them as free from underwood as if it had been carefully uprooted. This is attributed to the practice of the Indians to kindle fires year after year upon these grass-grown fields, whereby the bushes and trees were destroyed; and it is not many years since the Indians were possessed of this tract of country.

As we proceeded, however, the land became a little more cultivated. One saw here and there a rudely-built log-house, with its fields of maize around it, and also of new-sown wheat. We then reached a vast billowy prairie, Liberty Prairie, as it is called, which seemed interminable, for our horses were tired, and evening was coming on; nor was it till late and in darkness that we reached Kos[h]konong, and our Norwegian driver, who came from that place, drove us to the house of the Norwegian pastor. This, too, was merely a small log-house.

The Norwegian pastor, Mr. P[reus], had only left Norway to come hither a few months before. His young and pretty wife was standing in the kitchen, where a fire was blazing, boiling groats as I entered. I accosted her in Swedish. She was amazed at first, and terrified by the late visit, as her husband was from home on an official journey, and she was here quite alone with her little brother and an old woman servant; but she received us with true Northern hospitality and good-will, and she was ready to do every thing in the world to entertain and accommodate us.

As the house was small, and its resources not very ample, Mrs. C. and her sister drove to the house of an American farmer who lived at some little distance, I remaining over night with the little Norwegian lady. She was only nineteen, sick at heart for her mother, her home, and the mountains of her native land, now was happy in this strange country, and in those new circumstances to which she was so little accustomed. . . .

The young lady gave me a remarkably good tea, and a good bed in her room; but a terrific thunder-storm which prevailed through the whole night, with torrents of rain, disturbed our rest, especially that of my little hostess, who was afraid, and sighed over the life in "this disagreeable country."

Next morning the sun shone, the air was pleasant and mild; and after breakfast with the young lady, during which I did all in my power to inspire her with better feelings toward the country, and a better heart, I went out for a ramble. The parsonage, with all its homely thriftiness, was, nevertheless, beautifully situated upon a hill, surrounded by young oaks. The place, with a little care, may be made pretty and excellent. I wandered along the road; the country, glowing with sunshine, opened before me like an immense English park, with a background of the most beautiful arable land, fringed with leafy woods, now splendid with the colors of autumn. Here and there I saw little farm-houses, built on the skirts of the forest, mostly of log-houses; occasionally, however, might be seen a frame house, as well as small gray stone cottages. I saw the people out in the fields busied with their corn-harvest. I addressed them in Norwegian, and they joyfully fell into conversation.

I asked many, both men and women, whether they were contented — whether they were better off here than in old Norway? Nearly all of them replied "*Yes*. We are better off here; we do not work so hard, and it is easier to gain a livelihood." One old peasant only said, "There are difficulties here as well as there. The health is better in the old country than it is here!"

I visited also, with Mrs. P[reus], some of the Norwegian peasant houses. It may be that I did not happen to go into the best of them; but certainly the want of neatness and order I found contrasted strongly with the condition of the poor American cottages. But the Norwegians wisely built their houses generally beside some little river or brook, and understand how to select a good soil. They come hither as old and accustomed agriculturists, and know how to make use of the earth. They help one another in their labor, live frugally, and ask for no pleasures. The land seems to me, on all hands, to be rich, and has an idyllian beauty. Mountains there are none; only swelling hills, crowned with pine-wood. About seven hundred Norwegian colonists are settled in this neighborhood, all upon small farms, often at a great distance from one another. There are two churches, or meeting-houses, at Kos[h]ko-nong. . . .

It is said to be difficult to give to one portion of these Norwegian people any sense of religious or civil order; they are spoken of as obstinate and unmanageable; but they are able tillers of the ground, and they prepare the way for a better race; and their children, when they have been taught in American schools, and after that become servants in the better American families, are praised as the best of servants — faithful, laborious, and attached; merely difficult to accustom to perfect cleanliness and order. The greater number of domestic servants in these young Mississippi States come from the Norwegian colonies scattered over the country. In a general way, the Norwegians seem to succeed better here than the Swedes. A Norwegian newspaper is published at Madison, called *The Norwegian's Friend*, some copies of which I have obtained.

After an excellent breakfast, at which our young hostess, at my request, regaled us also with songs of her native land, sung to the guitar with fresh, sweet voice, we took our leave of that amiable lady, who will now find a good friend in Mrs. C., and, through her, many other friends in Madison. We drove home in a shower of rain, stopping now and then by the way to talk with the Norwegian people in the fields, and reached Madison as the sun sank amid the most unimaginable splendor, over that beautiful lake district and the city. The prevalence of sunny weather in America makes it easier, and more agreeable, to travel there than any where else. One may be sure of fine weather; and if a heavy shower does come, you may depend upon its soon being over, and that the sun will shortly be out again.

In Madison I have seen a good many people, and some tiresome interrogators (and these I place among the goats), with the usual questions, "How do you like the United States? How do you like Madison? Our roads? Do you know Jenny Lind personally?" and so on. Some interesting and unusually agreeable people I also saw (and these I place among the sheep), who have enough to say without living by questions, and who afforded me some hours of very interesting conversation.

Foremost among these I must mention the Chancellor of the University of Wisconsin, Mr. Lathrop, an agreeable and really intellectual man, full of life, and a clear and intelligent sense of the value of that youthful state in the group of the United States, and their common value in the history of the world. I derived much pleasure from his conversation, and from the perusal of a speech which he made a short time since in the Capitol here, on his installation as Chancellor of the University. This, together with another speech on the same occasion, by Mr. Hyatt Smith, one of the directors of the Educational Committee, shows a great understanding of the social relationship in general, and of that of the New World in particular; of the relationship of the past with the present, and of the present with the future, and both speeches breathe the noblest spirit. . . .

. . . Wisconsin has no hills, but on all sides uncultivated, and for the most part fertile land, abounding in lakes and rivers. It is a state for agriculture and the rearing of cattle; the land in many parts, however, and in particular around Madison, where it is to be appropriated by the Federal government to the supplying an income to the state's University, is already very dear. It has been purchased by speculators at the government price, a dollar and a quarter per acre, and resold by them for not less than ten or twelve dollars per acre.

"And who will give so much for it?" inquired I of Chancellor Lathrop.

"Your countrymen," replied he, quickly. "Your countrymen, whose sons will be freely educated at our University."

I visited, in company with Chancellor Lathrop and his cheerful, intelligent wife, the University which is now in progress of erection, and which will now be soon finished. It stands upon an elevation, "College Hill," as it is called, and which commands an open and extensive view; it is a large building, without any unnecessary pomp of exterior, as in Girard College at Philadelphia, but internally it has ample and spacious room. Many of the windows struck me, lighted up, as they were, by the setting sun. Such, after all, ought the Temple of the Sun to be on the

Western prairies! And if it fulfills its expectation, a Temple of the Light in spirit and in truth, more glorious than that of Peru!

It is only a few years since the Indians dwelt around these beautiful lakes; and they still come hither annually in the autumn to visit the graves of their ancestors, and to lift up their cry of lamentation!

BLUE MOUND(S)

I now write to you from a little log-house, in the midst of the prairie-land, between Madison and Galena. The log-house belongs to a farm, and is, at the same time, post-house, and a sort of country inn. Mr. D[ean], the son-in-law of my good hostess in Madison, had the kindness to drive me hither himself, in a little carriage, by which means I made the journey much more comfortably than by the stage, which comes here in the night.

Blue Mound[s] is one of the highest hills in Wisconsin, and derives its name from its fine dark blue color when seen from afar. It appears then as if enveloped in a clear purple veil, and is seen at many miles' distance, shrinking out thus against the soft blue sky. It resembles Kimkulle with us, but is more steep; like Kimkulle, it is covered with pasture-fields and wood.

When I arrived here I was so enchanted with the vast, glorious landscape, and with the view which it afforded over the prairie on all sides, that I resolved to remain here for a couple of days, in order that I might, in peace and solitude, become acquainted with the prairie and the sunflowers.

The house possessed but one guest chamber, and that a little garret within a large garret, in which were lodged half a dozen laboring men. But I was assured that they were very silent and well-behaved, and I was furnished with a piece of wood, with which to fasten the hasp of my door inside, as there was no lock. The room was clean and light, although very low and badly arranged; and I was glad to take up my abode in it, spite of the break-neck steps by which it was reached.

I spent nearly the whole of yesterday out in the prairie, now wandering over it, and gazing out over its infinite extent, which seemed, as it were, to expand and give wings to body and soul; and now sitting among sunflowers and asters, beside a little hillock covered with bushes, reading Emerson, that extraordinary Ariel, refreshing, but evanescent, and evanescent in his philosophic flights as the fugitive wing which sweeps across the prairie, and brings forth from the strings of the electric telegraph melodious tones, which sound and die away at the same moment. . . .

How grand is the impression produced by this infinite expanse of plain, with its solitude and its silence! In truth, it enables the soul to expand and grow, to have a freer and deeper respiration. That great West! Yes, indeed; but what solitude! I saw no habitations except the little house at which I was staying; no human beings, no animals; nothing except heaven and the flower-strewn earth. The day was beautiful and warm, and the sun advanced brightly through heaven and over earth, until toward evening, when by degrees it hid itself in light clouds of sun-smoke, which, as it descended, formed belts, through which the fiery globe shone with softened splendor, so that it represented a vast pantheon, with a cupola of gold, standing on the horizon above the immeasurable plain. This Temple of the Sun was to me one which I shall never forget.

To-morrow or the day following I shall leave this place and on Monday I hope to be on the Mississippi.

I shall now write a few words to young Mrs. D[ean] my beloved sunflower at Madison. I must tell you that the cook in her family, a respectable, clever Norwegian, would not on any terms receive money from me for the trouble she had had on my account.

THE LOG-HOUSE

It was cloudy this morning, and I was afraid of rain; but for all that, I went out "*à la bonne aventure.*" And to set out thus by one's self is so delightful. I followed a little path which wound through low boscage over the prairie. I there met some little children, who, with their mat-baskets in their hands, were wandering along to school. I accompanied them, and came to a little house built also of logs, and extremely humble. This was the school-house. The school-room was merely a room in which were some benches; the children, about a dozen in number, were ragged — regular offspring of the wilderness. But they seemed willing enough to learn; and upon the log walls of the room hung maps of the globe, upon which the young scholars readily pointed out to me the countries I mentioned; and there were also in that poor school-house such books as the "National Geography," by Goodrich, Smith's "Quarto Geography," which contains views of the whole world; while in the reading book in common use I found gems from the literature of all countries, and particularly from that of England and North America. The schoolmaster was an agreeable young man. His monthly stipend was fifteen dollars.

I went onward, the sun broke through the clouds; the day became glorious, and again I spent a lovely day alone on the prairie.

The host and hostess of my log-house are of Dutch origin, and not without education. The food is simple, but good; I can have as much excellent milk and potatoes as I desire (without spice or fat, and potatoes in this country are my best food), as well as capital butter and bread. Every thing is clean in the house, but the furniture and the conveniences are not superior to such as are to be met with in common Swedish peasant-houses. I sit at table with the men and maid-servants of the family, just as they come in from their work, and not over clean, as well as with thousands of flies.

The further I advance into the West the earlier become the hours of the meals. What do you say to breakfasting at six in the morning, dining at twelve, and having tea at half past six in the evening? I do not dislike it. It is a thousand times better than the fashionable hours for meals in New York and Boston.

It is evening. It has begun to rain and blow, and it is no easy thing to keep the wind and rain out of the window, which I am sometimes obliged to open on account of the oppressive heat occasioned by an iron pipe, which goes through the room from an iron stove in the room below. I am beginning to feel not quite so comfortable, and shall be glad to go in the morning to Galena. As far as my neighbors are concerned, I do not hear a sound of them, so silent are they. Log-houses are in general warm, but very dusty; so at least I have heard many people say, and I can myself believe it.

GALENA

You now find me here, a few miles from the great Mississippi, in a little town, picturesquely situated among hills beside a little river, called Five River [Fever River], which, with many sinuosities, winds through the glens. The town is supported by its lead mines, which are general in this highland district; by mining, smelting, and the export of this heavy, dark metal. A leaden sky hung over the town as I entered it, and I see in the street old madams waddling about in dull gray-colored cloaks and old bonnets, very much like poor old madams in shabby bonnets and cloaks in the streets of Stockholm in gray autumn weather; gentlemen too, or semi-gentlemen, in ragged coats — but less annoyed by them than they would be with us. Every thing looks dolefully gray; and it is as cold as it is in November with us. Yesterday it was quite otherwise. Yesterday was a most glorious summer day.

It rained when at dawn I left Blue Mound[s], but soon afterward cleared up; the wind chased the clouds across the immense plain, and the play of light and shadow over it, and those glorious views — I can not express how much I enjoyed that day's journey! The road along that high prairie-land was hard and level as the roads with us in summer. The diligence in which I sat, for the most part alone, rolled lightly across the plain, and seemed to fly over it, approaching every moment nearer to the giant river, the western goal of my journey. The wind was as warm as with us in July; and these western views, which increased in grandeur the nearer we approached the great river, produced an unspeakable effect. I never experienced any thing similar produced by a natural object.

FOR FURTHER READING

Arden, G. Everett. *Augustana Heritage: A History of the Augustana Lutheran Church.* Rock Island, Illinois: Augustana College, 1962.

Barton, H. Arnold (ed.). *Letters from the Promised Land: Swedes in America, 1840–1914.* Minneapolis: University of Minnesota Press for the Swedish Pioneer Historical Society, 1975.

Ehn, Erik. "The Swedes in Wisconsin: Concerning Source Material on the Study of Early Swedish Immigration to Wisconsin," *Swedish Pioneer Historical Quarterly, XIX.* April 1968, 116–129.

Friman, Axel. "Notes on a Wisconsin Pioneer," *Swedish Pioneer Historical Quarterly, XIII.* January 1962, 5–8.

Kastrup, Allan. *The Swedish Heritage in America: The Swedish Element in America and American-Swedish Relations in Their Historical Perspective.* St. Paul, Minnesota: Swedish Council of America, 1975.

Ljungmark, Lars. *Swedish Exodus.* Carbondale and Edwardsville, Illinois: Southern Illinois University Press for the Swedish Pioneer Historical Society, 1979.

Margulies, Herbert F. *Senator Lenroot of Wisconsin: A Political Biography, 1900–1929.* Columbia: University of Missouri Press, 1977.

Nelson, Helge. *The Swedes and Swedish Settlements in North America,* 2 vols. Lund: C. W. K. Gleerup, 1943.

Runblom, Harald and Hans Norman (eds.). *From Sweden to America: A History of the Migration. A Collective Work of the Uppsala Migration Research Project.* Minneapolis and Uppsala: University of Minnesota Press and Acta Universitatis Upsaliensis, University of Uppsala.

Stephenson, George M. *The Religious Aspects of Swedish Immigration.* Minneapolis: University of Minnesota Press, 1932.

Unonius, Gustaf. *A Pioneer in Northwest America, 1841–1858: The Memoirs of Gustaf Unonius,* 2 vols. Minneapolis: University of Minnesota Press for the Swedish Pioneer Historical Society, 1950, 1960.

THE AUTHOR

FREDERICK HALE (born 1948) graduated from Macalester College in 1969 and was awarded master's degrees at Harvard University, the University of Minnesota, and the Johns Hopkins University. He received his Doctor of Philosophy at Johns Hopkins in 1976. In addition to Swedes in Wisconsin he has written five books in the field of Scandinavian immigration and has contributed articles to historical, literary, and theological journals in the United Kingdom, Scandinavia, Africa, and the United States.

INDEX